ANIMAL SUPERSTARS

And More True Stories of Amazing Animal Talents

Published by the National Geographic Society
John M. Fahey, *Chairman of the Board and Chief Executive Officer*
Timothy T. Kelly, *President*
Declan Moore, *Executive Vice President; President, Publishing and Digital Media*
Melina Gerosa Bellows, *Executive Vice President; Chief Creative Officer, Books, Kids, and Family*

Prepared by the Book Division
Hector Sierra, *Senior Vice President and General Manager*
Nancy Laties Feresten, *Senior Vice President, Kids Publishing and Media*
Jonathan Halling, *Design Director, Books and Children's Publishing*
Jay Sumner, *Director of Photography, Children's Publishing*
Jennifer Emmett, *Vice President, Editorial Director, Children's Books*
Eva Absher-Schantz, *Design Director, Kids Publishing and Media*
Carl Mehler, *Director of Maps*
R. Gary Colbert, *Production Director*
Jennifer A. Thornton, *Director of Managing Editorial*

Staff for This Book
Becky Baines, *Project Editor*
Lisa Jewell, *Illustrations Editor*
Eva Absher-Schantz, *Art Director*
Ruthie Thompson, *Designer*
Grace Hill, *Associate Managing Editor*
Joan Gossett, *Production Editor*
Marfé Ferguson Delano, *Release Editor*
Lewis R. Bassford, *Production Manager*
Susan Borke, *Legal and Business Affairs*
Kate Olesin, *Assistant Editor*
Kathryn Robbins, *Associate Designer*
Hillary Moloney, *Illustrations Assistant*

Manufacturing and Quality Management
Phillip L. Schlosser, *Senior Vice President*
Chris Brown, *Vice President, NG Book Manufacturing*
George Bounelis, *Vice President, Production Services*
Nicole Elliott, *Manager*
Rachel Faulise, *Manager*
Robert L. Barr, *Manager*

The National Geographic Society is one of the world's largest nonprofit scientific and educational organizations. Founded in 1888 to "increase and diffuse geographic knowledge," the Society's mission is to inspire people to care about the planet. It reaches more than 400 million people worldwide each month through its official journal, *National Geographic,* and other magazines; National Geographic Channel; television documentaries; music; radio; films; books; DVDs; maps; exhibitions; live events; school publishing programs; interactive media; and merchandise. National Geographic has funded more than 10,000 scientific research, conservation, and exploration projects and supports an education program promoting geographic literacy.

For more information, please visit www.nationalgeographic.com, call 1-800-NGS LINE (647-5463), or write to the following address:
National Geographic Society
1145 17th Street N.W.
Washington, D.C. 20036-4688 U.S.A.

Visit us online at www.nationalgeographic.com/books

For librarians and teachers: www.ngchildrensbooks.org

More for kids from National Geographic: kids.nationalgeographic.com

For information about special discounts for bulk purchases, please contact National Geographic Books Special Sales: ngspecsales@ngs.org

For rights or permissions inquiries, please contact National Geographic Books Subsidiary Rights: ngbookrights@ngs.org

Trade paperback
ISBN: 978-1-4263-1091-1
Reinforced library edition
ISBN: 978-1-4263-1092-8

Printed in China
12/RRDS/1

Table of CONTENTS

OPEE: THE MOTOCROSS BIKER PUP

Opee and Mike
Schelin go
airborne! They
both love to ride
Mike's dirt bike.

Ready to ride, Opee pants with excitement. His helmet has a camera on top.

Chapter 1

EASY RIDER

April 2006, San Diego, California

Opee the Australian (sounds like AH-STRALE-YAN) shepherd cocks his head and listens. Has Mike entered the garage? The devoted dog jumps to his feet and runs toward the sound. Barking excitedly, he leaps onto the gas tank of Mike Schelin's dirt bike. Opee's pink tongue hangs out. His front paws rest on the handlebars.

Mike grins. He slips a helmet and goggles on the happy dog's head. He hops on the bike behind Opee and kicks the starter with his heel. Off they go across the California desert.

Mike is a professional motocross (sounds like MOE-TOE-CROSS) racer. And so is Opee! Motocross is a form of cross-country motorcycle racing. Racers ride special motocross bikes, also called dirt bikes. They race on rugged tracks that are closed to normal traffic.

Mike and Opee's story started when Mike Schelin was 35 years old. Things had not been going well for him lately and he was unhappy. *Cheer up!* he told himself. But he didn't know how. So he sat down with a pad and pencil.

He made a list of all the things that made him feel good.

Later Mike read what he wrote. *Hmm,* he thought, *dogs are first on my list. I need a job that lets me bring a dog to work.*

Soon Mike quit his job selling computers and moved to San Diego, California. He met a man there who let Mike live in an old house for free. In return, Mike agreed to fix up the place. But something was missing. Mike needed a dog to keep him company.

He called a woman who had an Australian shepherd puppy for sale. They agreed to meet on a country road where 75 mailboxes stood in a row.

Mike spotted the mailboxes first. Then he saw a mother dog and puppy playing in the grass. The puppy had soft, floppy ears. His furry coat had patches of black, brown, and gray with white around his neck. His eyes were different colors. One was blue and the other was brown. Mike scooped him up, and slurp! The little furball stuck out his tongue and licked Mike's face. Mike paid the woman and drove home with the puppy.

Mike didn't think of the dog as a pet. He thought of him more as a friend, or even a brother. He named the pup Opee, his own nickname as a child.

The next day, Mike woke up to whining. "Are you hungry, fella?" Mike asked. He poured some kibble into a plastic bowl and fixed himself a cup of coffee.

The house was a mess. A table saw stood in the middle of the living room. Rows of bare wooden studs rose like jail bars at one end of the room. Piles of sweet-smelling sawdust littered the floor.

Mike grabbed a hammer and started to work. Opee followed behind, leaving paw prints in the dust. Later he curled up in Mike's toolbox to sleep.

One day, Mike and Opee drove to the hardware store for supplies. When they got there, Mike set the puppy on a flatbed cart. "Stay," he said. Opee did. Mike was surprised by how well he obeyed. "He just seemed to get it," Mike said.

On weekends, Mike relaxed by riding his dirt bike in the desert. He took Opee with him. Mike thought Opee would enjoy running off-leash. Maybe he'd run after lizards and snakes. But Opee chased Mike instead. He chased him uphill and downhill. Over bumps and pits and in clouds of dust. The dog never stopped.

Mike decided to buy a quad—a four-wheeled off-road motorbike with a seat big enough for two. Now Opee could ride along! But how to keep the dust out of Opee's eyes? Mike had an idea. First he cut a slit in the middle of a sock. Then he slipped a pair of goggles through the slit and tied the ends of the sock under Opee's chin. Perfect! Opee jumped onto the seat and off they went.

Motorbikes are loud. Other dogs might have hated the noise. They might have jumped off the seat in fear. Not Opee.

One Sunday Mike didn't go to the desert. Instead, he wanted to ride his street bike to Santa Barbara, another city in California. His street bike is a big, rumbling Harley-Davidson motorcycle. Mike hadn't ridden the Harley in a while. So he took it for a test-drive around the block.

"Opee was at the gate going crazy," Mike said. "He was barking and jumping." The minute Mike let his dog loose, Opee surprised him by jumping up on the gas tank. "Okay," Mike said, hugging his dog. "I'll take you for a spin."

Mike started slow. The dog didn't blink. Mike went faster. The dog stayed put. When the speed reached 50 miles an hour (81 km/h), Opee crouched down closer to the bike. When the road curved, Opee leaned into the turns. *This dog is a natural,* Mike thought.

Mike hurried home and dashed into the house. Grabbing his extra helmet, he sawed a chunk out of the back so it would fit around Opee's head. Then he put the helmet, goggles, and a backpack on the pup. They were about to leave when Mike had another thought. He found some rope and tied Opee to him, just in case the dog lost his balance.

To Santa Barbara and back is 300 miles (483 km)—a long trip on a motorcycle. Mike wondered how long Opee would last.

Surprise! Opee made it the entire way.

Feeling Upset?

Get a pup.
Dogs understand
when people are
nervous or scared. Seeing
you cry makes a dog feel bad. It will tuck
its tail and bow its head, say scientists at
the University of London, in England. A
dog will snuggle against you and give you
a doggie hug. You can bury your face in
its soft fur, and it will lick your cheek.

Pretty soon, you will stop thinking
about yourself and think about your pup
instead. You might even smile.

Mike and his loyal canine partner look sharp riding the hills.

Chapter 2

UPPING the STAKES

The next weekend, Mike and Opee returned to the desert. This time Opee walked right past the quad and jumped on Mike's dirt bike. Riding a dirt bike is harder than riding a motorcycle or quad. Keeping balance over bumps is difficult and tiring. Mike decided to take Opee for a test spin. No problem! Soon they were riding longer and faster than Mike's motocross pals.

Other riders urged Mike to enter the Lake Elsinore Grand Prix (sounds like PREE) with Opee. Forty years ago, a popular movie was made about this 100-mile (161-km) motocross race. Today nearly 1,000 people compete in it.

But riding for fun in the desert is one thing. Competitive racing is quite another. "They won't let a dog in that race," Mike said.

"Sure they will," insisted his friends. "They let someone else do it once."

Mike agreed to give it a try. The first thing he did was take Opee shopping. Nobody sold motocross gear for dogs. But Mike bought Opee the best-fitting helmet, goggles, and padded jersey he could find.

On a chilly November morning, Mike and Opee drove to Lake Elsinore, California. They reported to the check-in table. Mike paid the race fee and signed them up. He picked up two wristbands and three white signs with his number on them. He carefully attached the signs to his dirt bike. He slipped on one wristband and slid the other onto Opee's front leg.

Mike checked his gas and warmed up his engine. Opee hopped on and Mike drove slowly toward the raceway. The crowd separated to let them through the gate.

Mike gasped at the dazzling sight of row upon row of helmeted riders dressed in padded suits. Every rider sat on a brightly colored dirt bike with bumpy tires. It looked like a lineup from a parade. To be safe, Mike and Opee

took a place in the back. The race can get
rough. Accidents happen. Mike didn't
want to put Opee at risk.

A woman carrying a clipboard walked up
and down the lines. She inspected each bike
and rider. Were they registered? Were they
wearing the proper gear? When the woman
reached Mike and Opee, she smiled. Still
smiling, she went down her list. Check.
Check. Mike and Opee passed inspection.

As everyone waited for the race to begin,
some of the riders bounced on their seats.
Others talked or laughed nervously. Mike
squeezed and released his hand brakes.
Opee sat patiently and barely moved.

Finally, a man yelled through a
bullhorn. The race was starting! Another
man standing on a platform waved a green

flag. The first row of riders roared away. Each one left a burst of smoke behind. The flag waved again and again. Row after row of racers sped off. Mike and Opee's row was coming up soon. Mike leaned forward and shifted his weight.

The flag came down. They were off!

The uphill track immediately changed to dirt. Mike saw hay bales and a string of colored flags ahead. It was a corner. He and Opee leaned into it. Mike slowed and stuck his leg out for balance. A rider ahead of them went too fast. His bike crashed in the dirt. Mike jerked the handlebars and swerved around him.

The entire route was closed to traffic. Only racers could use it today. But the raceway kept changing. First it was dirt.

Then it was pavement. Then dirt again. It went uphill and down. It twisted and turned. For a while it wound right through the center of town.

Clusters of men and women stood on the grass bordering the route. Little kids in baseball caps perched on their fathers' shoulders. Everyone turned toward the roar of the bikes. As the riders whizzed by, the people cheered. "Hey, look!" someone yelled. "There's a dog in the race!"

People waved and shouted. The cheering grew louder when Mike and Opee rode by. Mike had never heard anything like it. He felt like a rock star.

Race officials stood at checkpoints along the way. They waved yellow flags to warn riders of turns and intersections.

Doggie Daredevils

Motocross is dangerous. People can get hurt or killed. That's why motocross is called an "extreme sport." Besides competing against others, extreme sport athletes also battle nature. They may face fierce winds, giant waves, snow, ice, finger-numbing cold, or blistering heat. Contestants need both physical and mental strength.

Dogs take part in extreme sports, too. The best known event is the Iditarod (sounds like EYE-DIT-ur-ODD). Held in Alaska, it's an 1,100-mile (1,770-km) race for sled dogs. The winners of that truly are "top dogs."

Crashes happened anyway. Rescue vehicles patrolled the track. They towed trailers to pick up broken bikes and bring them back. Ambulances stood by to help.

The race was a test of skill. It was more about staying power than speed. "We're not in it to win," Mike told himself. "We just want to finish." Even so, he and Opee passed 100 riders along the way.

Mike and Opee made it to the checkered flag at the finish line and sputtered to a stop. Mike yanked off their helmets and threw an arm around his partner. "Good dog, Opee," he said and kissed his pal's wet, black nose. "Good dog!"

This dog is special, Mike thought. *This dog can make a difference*. Right then and there Mike set a new goal. He would use

Opee to help people. He would take him to hospitals to visit sick kids. He would register him as a therapy dog. But first Mike wanted Opee to do something no other dog had ever done. He decided to enter them in the most challenging motocross race of all—the Baja (sounds like BA-HA) 500 in Mexico.

The Baja 500 was expensive. Race fees alone were almost a thousand dollars. Then there was food, hotels, and gasoline to pay for. Mike knew he couldn't afford it on his own. He needed a sponsor. Sponsors are people or companies who help pay an athlete's expenses. In return, the athlete wears clothes and uses equipment that advertises the sponsor's name. But how would Mike ever find such a deal?

Mud is no match for Mike and Opee, who love to get dirty on the course.

Chapter 3

RACE to Fame

Lucky for Mike and Opee, they had already met the person who would become their sponsor. It happened at the Lake Elsinore motocross race. As Mike and Opee zipped around the track that day, all of a sudden... *CLANK!* Mike looked over his shoulder and saw his muffler lying in the dirt! He pulled off to the side and skidded to a stop. "Stay," he told Opee.

Mike ran and picked up the muffler. The metal was so hot it melted his leather gloves. "Ouch!" Mike dropped the muffler and stood there feeling defeated. Without the muffler, the noise of his engine would be deafening.

A stranger came to the rescue. He threw a bucket of water on the muffler to cool it. Someone else handed Mike a shoelace. Mike used it to tie the muffler to his bike. Then he and Opee got back into the race and finished it.

Afterward Mike met the stranger who had helped him. His name was Marty Mooks, and he was a former motocross racer. Marty fell in love with Opee. He decided he wanted to help Opee and Mike race together. Marty gave Mike a new muffler and helped him get sponsors. These sponsors gave Mike free dog food, racing equipment, and money to help him compete.

The Baja 500 was a very different race from Lake Elsinore. At Lake Elsinore racers drove around and around the same track. At Baja they never covered the same ground twice. At nearly 500 miles (805 km), the Baja was also five times longer. Racers needed a cell phone in case they got lost. They also needed a chase vehicle to carry food and water for them. And unlike Lake Elsinore, Baja had a time limit. Racers had to finish within 18 hours.

But the biggest difference was that not only dirt bikes competed at Baja. People also raced four-wheeled bikes called ATVs, stripped-down automobiles with special tires, street motorcycles, cars, and trucks. Some of the trucks were as big and powerful as monster trucks.

Baja was scary. Riders had to pay attention every second. Mike decided that he and Opee couldn't do it alone. They would race as a team. Three of Mike's friends offered to help: a teenage boy, an army sergeant (sounds like SAR-JENT), and another motocross racer. They would run the race in relays. Everyone would take a turn on the dirt bike. But Opee and Mike would ride the longest.

The five-member team traveled to Mexico in Mike's old van. Once there, the men packed the van with supplies and prepared Mike's bike. They changed the oil and tuned up the engine. They checked the tires and brakes. They tested the lights. They made sure everything ran perfectly. Nobody wanted a breakdown in the desert.

Mike worked with Opee. He had been teaching him voice commands. Now they practiced again. "Set it up," Mike said, when they came to a jump. The dog instantly dropped down so Mike could see over his head.

> **Did You Know?**
>
> In some places, Australian shepherds are used to herd sheep and cattle.

At the bottom of a steep, sandy hill, Mike stopped the bike. He knew the bike could flip over backward as it climbed up. "Get off," he told Opee. Opee leaped to the ground. Mike gunned the engine and roared toward the top. Opee ran and got there first.

Mike stopped, the dog jumped back on, and off they went. Mike smiled. *We're ready*, he thought.

On race day, Opee looked like a pro. He wore a special doggie helmet with a camera on it. He also wore padding around his neck and a high-tech, inflatable chest protector. The human members of his team also wore special protective gear.

It was a good thing they did, too. The Baja was wilder than the craziest roller coaster ride. It had uphills, downhills, rocks, sand pits, mud holes, dust, and deep ditches. Mike's teenage friend only lasted 28 miles (45 km). The sergeant gave up after 60 (97 km). The other motocross racer made it 150 (241 km). But Mike and Opee? They just kept going, mile after mile, hour after hour.

Just before dark, Mike and Opee were riding fast. Mike wanted to reach the beach before the sun went down. He squeezed the gas. The speedometer spun. And then it happened. They were zooming along at an amazing 75 miles an hour (121 km/h) when they hit a silt bed. "A silt bed is like riding through flour," said Mike. "It will swallow your bike."

The back end of the bike spun out. It crashed to the ground. Both Mike and Opee flew through the air. Mike landed on his face in the dirt with his arms straight out in front of him. `Opee rolled to a stop near him.

Groaning, Mike climbed to his knees and crawled to his dog. He checked him for injuries. Opee had a scrape on his nose and another on his paw. Nothing serious, thank goodness. Mike sighed with relief.

Only then did he notice the blood. It was running into his boot from a cut on his calf.

It was decision time. Should they continue or drop out now? Mike was still thinking when Opee decided for him. The determined dog jumped back on the bike.

That day Mike and Opee rode for over 200 teeth-rattling miles (322 km). They reached the finish line with ten minutes to spare. Opee became the first dog ever to complete the Baja 500!

"It was the hardest thing I've done in my life," Mike said. "And I couldn't have done it without my dog."

Opee just wagged his tail.

Emergency!

Suppose your dog got hurt. Having a doggie first-aid kit would help. Here are some things to put in it. Make sure to have an adult help you if your pet really does get hurt.

1. Phone numbers for your local vet, an emergency vet clinic, and a poison control center
2. A list of your dog's medicines and shots
3. A muzzle or strips of cloth for tying the dog's mouth shut. (A hurt animal might bite.)
4. Nonstick bandages
5. Medical tape
6. Cornstarch to put on bleeding toenails
7. Blanket or towels

Sidewinder, a.k.a. Dunkirk Dave, is a small, female groundhog. She was found in this basket.

SIDEWINDER:
GROUNDHOG WEATHER WONDER

Like this one, most groundhogs are brown and gray. But some are black or even white.

Chapter 1

STAYING ALIVE

April 2005, Dunkirk, New York

A wounded baby groundhog trembled in fear. Someone had wrapped her in a blanket and put her in a basket. Just hours before, she and her brothers and sisters were probably eating dandelions in a grassy field. Now her siblings were gone. Her mother was nowhere to be seen. The terrified baby was all alone.

Meanwhile, Bob Will was driving home from visiting his parents. The setting sun glowed red over Lake Erie as he pulled into his driveway.

Bob got out of his jeep and walked around to the front of his house. He saw a beat-up wicker basket propped against his screen door. "What's this?" he wondered as he peeked inside.

"Oh, no!" Another hurt animal!

Bob is a wildlife rehabilitator (sounds like REE-UH-BILL-UH-TAY-TER). A wildlife rehabilitator is a person who has been trained to help wild animals in need. Sometimes people dropped off hurt animals at Bob's house. Once it was a swan with a broken wing. Another time a blind turtle turned up on his front steps. But this little baby groundhog tore at Bob's heart. She reminded him of the very first groundhog he had ever saved.

Bob was ten years old then. He found an injured groundhog in a farmer's field and took it home. Someone had shot it. "That's a throwaway animal!" a nosy neighbor said. "What are you taking care of that for?"

The unkind words made Bob want to cry. "Every animal has a right to life," he said. "This groundhog did not deserve to be shot." At home, Bob taped bandages over the groundhog's wounds. He fed him sugar water with an eyedropper. The groundhog slowly got better. Months later, Bob released him back into the wild.

"That gave me a feeling of power," he said. "I had saved an animal's life."

Now it was fifty years later, and people were still shooting groundhogs because they dig holes and sometimes eat crops. Bob shook his head sadly and brought the basket inside. He set it down beside a tower of plastic animal carriers, called kennels (sounds like KEN-uls). Then he went through his bathroom medicine cabinet. As a wildlife rehabilitator, Bob kept that cabinet well stocked with medical supplies.

Bob was washing the groundhog when his roommate and helper, Bill Verge, arrived home. Bill saw blood in the bathwater. "What happened?" he asked.

"I found her on the doorstep," Bob said. "Somebody shot her."

Bill pitched in to help. He held the groundhog while Bob bandaged her head. The animal was so weak she couldn't open her eyes. Bill laid her on a towel and put her in a kennel. He packed hot water bottles around her to keep her warm.

That night Bob woke up every two hours to feed the baby groundhog. But during the day, he taught school. That's when Bill took over the feedings. Bill worked at home. He and Bob ran a side business repairing old typewriters. The money they earned from this business paid for animal food and supplies.

Between them, Bob and Bill cared for the baby groundhog around the clock. But the animal was so thin she looked like a sack of bones. When she lifted her head, it flopped.

Hungry, Hungry Groundhogs!

Groundhogs aren't called "hogs" for nothing. A single animal eats a pound (0.5 kg) of greens a day and can destroy a garden. To keep groundhogs out without harming them, try these tips:

1. Play a radio in the garden.
2. Ask an adult to put in lights and alarms.
3. Dig a ditch around the garden. Bury woven wire fencing in it one foot deep (0.3 m). This should leave about three feet (0.9 m) of fencing aboveground. Leave the top wobbly so groundhogs can't climb it.

All the little groundhog did was lie on her side with her feet pawing the air. Bob started calling her "the girl who can't walk." He decided to take her to the vet.

The vet set the tiny limp animal on his table. He parted her fur with his fingers and looked at her wound. He shone a light in her ears and gently pressed the bones in her legs. "Her wounds are clean," the vet said. "They are starting to heal."

Bob smiled.

But there was more to come. "The bullet has damaged her brain," the vet said. "I'm afraid she might not make it."

Bob's shoulders slumped. He scooped up his girl and went home. But he did not give up.

For two months straight Bob got up at night to squirt food into the groundhog's mouth. She ate a mixture of sweet potatoes and monkey biscuits that Bob ground up in a blender. Monkey biscuits are made of nuts and grain. They are rock-hard and good for a groundhog's teeth.

One day Bob laid his hand against the groundhog's belly. For the first time it felt round and plump. "Woo-hoo!" Bob whooped. "Our girl is going to make it!"

Now if only she could learn to walk.

Six months passed. One day Bob set "the girl who can't walk" on the floor with some other rescued groundhogs. At least she could hang out with her friends. But this little girl groundhog did more than that. She copied them and tried to stand up.

Bob watched as she pushed herself to her feet. He held his breath as she wobbled in place. And he groaned in disappointment when she toppled over.

Stand up. Fall down. Stand up. Fall down.

It went on like this for days. Bob could not believe how hard the little groundhog tried. She simply wouldn't give up.

Then one day she did it. The girl stayed standing!

A few days later she took a step. Then she took another and another. Bill chuckled as he watched her make up for lost time. "Our girl that can't walk," he joked, "is always on the run!"

There was just one problem. The damage she had suffered had jumbled the signals in her brain. The plucky little groundhog could only walk in circles.

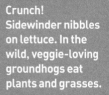

Crunch!
Sidewinder nibbles
on lettuce. In the
wild, veggie-loving
groundhogs eat
plants and grasses.

Chapter 2

GROUNDHOG DAY!

ob and Bill finally named the little groundhog. They called her "Sidewinder" because she couldn't walk straight. Bob looked at her sleeping in her kennel one night. He noticed that she held a corner of a towel in her mouth. *How come?* he wondered. Then he heard a soft sucking sound. "Bill, come here," Bob whispered.

Bill tiptoed over. He looked and listened. He heard it, too. The little groundhog was sucking on the towel. It was just like a baby sucking on a pacifier.

Now that Sidewinder could stand, she could eat on her own. And boy, was she hungry! She crunched carrots. She gobbled up lettuce. She snacked on corn on the cob. And she topped it all off with lemon cake for dessert.

The trouble was that mealtimes took forever. Wild groundhogs sit while they chow down. Not Sidewinder. She took one bite of food. Then she walked in a circle. She took a second bite. She looped around again. Round and round she went.

Sometimes she walked through her food. Carrots and biscuits scattered all about. Much of it ended up uneaten.

This worried Bill. All that walking used up a lot of energy. Sidewinder needed to eat more food than other groundhogs, not less.

Bob and Bill had an idea. When it was time to eat, they put Sidewinder and her food inside a large box. There she had to walk in smaller circles. Now she could finish a meal in three hours. It no longer took all day.

Bob was proud of Sidewinder. She had overcome so much. Maybe she would be up for a new challenge—Groundhog Day.

Groundhog Day comes on February 2. That's right in the middle of winter. People are often tired of winter by then. They are eager for spring. They like having an excuse for a celebration. You can guess what animal this celebration is about!

Bob and Bill were in charge of finding the groundhogs used in New York State. It started back in 1967. That year Bob brought a rescued groundhog to school. He showed it to his students.

The school custodian got really excited. He called the newspaper. "Have I got a story for you!" he said.

The paper sent a reporter to school. The reporter named the groundhog Dunkirk Dave, after their town. He asked Bob if the groundhog could forecast the weather. Maybe Dunkirk Dave could be New York's version of Punxsutawney (sounds like PUNKS-SUH-TAW-NEE) Phil!

Phil was another groundhog. He lived indoors in a town called Punxsutawney, Pennsylvania. Every Groundhog Day a group of men brought him outside to forecast the weather.

This was an old idea. It first came from Germany. People there held a festival called Candlemas (sounds like KAN-DUHL-MAS) on February 2. Part of this holiday was about the weather. It also had to do with a furry animal called a badger (sounds like BAJ-ER). If the sun was bright enough on Candlemas, a badger would see its shadow. Uh-oh! That meant winter would last another six weeks. But if the day was cloudy the badger would not see its shadow. That meant, "Hello, spring!"

When people came from Germany to the United States, they could not find any badgers. They did find groundhogs. In the 1800s, farmers in Pennsylvania began using them instead. On February 2 they watched to see if a groundhog saw its shadow. They had a picnic the same day.

Every year the picnic got bigger. Newspapers printed stories about it. More people wanted to know if the groundhog saw its shadow. More states began to celebrate Groundhog Day. In New York, Dunkirk Dave became the star of the show.

But groundhogs only live about 15 years. So, many have played the part.

Wild Weather Quiz

Today computers help us forecast the weather. Long ago people watched animals for signs that the weather was changing. Here are some of those signs. Do you know which ones are true?

1. Pigs gather sticks before a storm.
2. Crickets chirp faster as it gets warmer.
3. Frogs croak louder and more often just before it rains.
4. When ladybugs swarm, expect a day that is warm.

Answer: They are all true.

"It is important to have a groundhog that is calm around people," Bob says. A scared one might bite somebody.

Bob thought Sidewinder might be perfect for the role. To find out, he took her to meet his students.

In Bob's class, all of the kids had special needs. It set them apart. Sometimes they felt left out. But all that changed when Bob brought Sidewinder into class. Everyone wanted to watch her turn circles. They got in line to hold and pet her. Sidewinder seemed to love everybody.

"What soft fur you have," said one girl.

"What big teeth!" said a boy.

Their excitement spread. "What's going on in Mr. Will's room?" asked a boy passing by in the hall. He took a peek.

Suddenly lots of kids wanted to come into the room. Sidewinder made Bob's students feel important.

In one way, she and they were alike. She also had disabilities (sounds like DIS-UH-BILL-UH-TEES) that made it hard for her to learn. Bob explained how Sidewinder kept trying. She never gave up. Her story gave the kids hope. If they kept trying, maybe they could do things that were hard for them, too.

At the end of the day Bob smiled to himself. Sidewinder did not get scared around strangers. She kept her cool. He thought she would make a great Dunkirk Dave come Groundhog Day.

> **Did You Know?**
>
> When scared, groundhogs give a high whistle. That's why they're also called "whistle pigs."

On Groundhog Day, an antique dollhouse sets the stage for Sidewinder to play the role of Dunkirk Dave.

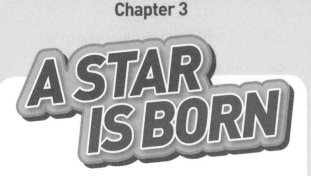

Chapter 3

A STAR IS BORN

Groundhog Day finally rolled around. At last it was Sidewinder's big day! Bob and Bill got up long before sunrise. Bill tended to the squirrels and other animals they cared for. He filled their water dishes and fed them. He changed their bedding and gave them medicine. Suddenly he heard a loud clanking noise. It was coming from Sidewinder's kennel.

"Sounds like Sidewinder wants some food," Bill said.

"She probably does," said Bob, laughing. "But today she will just have to wait. She will get plenty to eat once the sun comes up."

Sidewinder kept up the racket. She banged and banged the heavy hook holding her kennel door shut. *CLANK! CLANK! CLANK! Where's my dinner? CLANK! CLANK! CLANK!*

The hook was not a dinner bell. But Sidewinder thought it was. She had learned this trick all on her own. One day she banged that hook and food appeared. Aha! She banged the hook another time and it happened again. The men realized what she wanted and fed her. Then Sidewinder began banging the hook whenever she was hungry. And Bob and Bill were happy to help, except for today.

This was the one day of the year when Sidewinder must be patient. Today she would play the role of Dunkirk Dave. It was up to her to pop out of the groundhog hole in Bob's backyard. A crowd of people would be there. Everyone would be eager to find out if the groundhog saw her shadow.

The day before Groundhog Day, Bob worried about something. The weather had been warm that winter, and the snow had melted in Bob's backyard. The ground was bare. Wild animals were out looking for food. Bob had spotted a fox close by. He also had seen a skunk. Either one might come poking around his yard. That would put Sidewinder in danger. Foxes and skunks eat groundhogs! Bob thought for a while about how to keep Sidewinder safe.

Then he remembered his mother's old dollhouse. Her father made it for her when she was a little girl. Bob found the toy and carried it into the backyard. He paused for a minute before setting it down. His grandpa had built the dollhouse almost one hundred years ago. *It is a shame to do this*, Bob thought. *But Mom would understand.*

He took a saw and cut a hole through the bottom of the dollhouse. He made the hole as big around as the groundhog hole. Then he sat the house over the top.

And now it was almost show time! Bob carried Sidewinder outdoors. "Our guests will be here any minute," he told her.

It was still black as night when Bob opened the dollhouse roof and put Sidewinder inside. When he closed it she was nice and safe. Behind the house stood a miniature windmill. A sign hung on the tower. It read "Dunkirk Dave."

Then Bob went back indoors and changed into his best suit. He carefully tied his tie and combed his hair. The smell of coffee filled the air as he put doughnuts and cups on a table. For the children he had a special treat. He had bought furry, groundhog finger puppets for them. They felt soft and cuddly like Sidewinder.

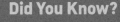

Did You Know?

Sometimes groundhogs gobble up insects, snails, and birds' eggs.

Groovy Groundhogs

1. Groundhogs are rodents, like mice and beavers.
2. A groundhog's teeth never stop growing.
3. Groundhogs are also called "woodchucks" and "marmots."
4. Groundhogs spend most of their lives underground.
5. Groundhogs mostly sleep in winter.
6. Groundhogs can swim.
7. Foxes, skunks, and snakes often move into abandoned groundhog burrows.
8. Groundhogs can climb trees.
9. Groundhogs love to lie in the sun.

Every kid who came to visit would get a puppet. Bob hoped this day would encourage people to stop thinking of groundhogs as throwaway animals. He hoped it would help stop people from killing them.

Bob heard the rumble of a car engine. He peeked out his sliding glass doors. A white news van had just arrived. Bob saw photographers, reporters, college students, parents, and schoolchildren gathered in his yard. He went to join them. Everyone was waiting for the sun to come up.

When it did, Bob knelt beside the dollhouse. He set a paper plate of lettuce and lemon cake on the ground. He put a finger to his lips. "Shh," he said.

The crowd went quiet. Bob knocked on the side of the dollhouse. A small brown head appeared at the window. One tiny eye looked out.

Bob jiggled the plate. "Have some lemon cake," he said.

Groundhogs can hear sounds that people can't. Sidewinder listened carefully. If she heard anything scary she would not come out.

Everyone waited.

Sidewinder twitched her whiskers. She turned her head. Her body stretched out like a sausage. POP! Sidewinder slipped through the window and out of the dollhouse.

She nibbled at the lemon cake.

Bob looked at the cloudy sky. He looked at Sidewinder. He did not see a shadow. "We're going to have an early spring," he said. The crowd cheered.

The television crew packed up their stuff. A few people came forward to pet Sidewinder and chat with Bob. Eventually the crowd left.

Sidewinder was a big hit as Dunkirk Dave. Now she's a star! Hundreds of people have watched her videos online. Thousands more have seen her picture. A reporter in California heard about the disabled groundhog and the men who cared for her. She flew across the country to write about them. Other newspapers reprinted her story. Now Bob, Bill, and Dunkirk Dave are known from coast to coast.

Maybe Sidewinder did run in circles, but her message was straight as an arrow. "Look at me," her actions said. "We groundhogs are well worth saving."

THE
ROCK

TH
RO
CA

These cool cats are ready to rock and roll! *MEEE-WOW!*

TUNA: KITTY ROCK STAR

Tuna looks ready to sing for her favorite treat. That's tuna fish, of course!

Born to PURR-FORM

Spring 2003, Chicago, Illinois

A white kitten with big green eyes sat on a cardboard box. She looked very cute. Her name was Tuna. She had just been plopped down in a place she didn't know. Bright lights shone down from metal poles. They made her fur hot to the touch. A panting dog waited his turn in a corner. Tuna was having her picture taken.

"Most kittens would run," said Tuna's owner. Her name is Samantha Martin. Samantha loves cats. In fact, she loves all animals. She studied the care and raising of them in college. She dreamed of training animals for television and movies. When a photographer needed a kitten for a pet food ad, she offered her cat Tuna for the job. Now the photographer gripped a heavy camera and circled Tuna like a hungry wolf.

Samantha held her breath. *Please, Tuna,* she thought. *Don't bolt.*

The brave kitten stayed. She held her pose like a supermodel.

"Great!" the photographer said. "I got some good shots."

Samantha beamed. She opened a can of tuna fish, and the little kitty gobbled it up.

Before she got Tuna, Samantha trained rats. Her personal zoo also included a raccoon that could play basketball and a groundhog that could raise a flag. She had also trained a chicken, a duck, and a goose to play tiny musical instruments. But none of these acts drew a large enough audience for Samantha to earn a living from them.

To make it in show business, Samantha needed to train more popular animals. Watching Tuna in action started her thinking. Cat actors were much in demand. Somebody had to provide them. Why not Samantha?

"Tuna," Samantha said. "We're going to make you a star."

The next day Samantha brought out more tuna fish. She gave Tuna a nibble.

Then she waggled a long stick in front of her.

Tuna leaped and pounced, chasing the stick. The second Tuna's paw hit the stick, Samantha snapped a clicker. Then she gave the cat a bit of fish. They did this several times. Then, flash! Tuna realized that the click meant food. She had to touch the stick to get it.

The next day, Samantha brought out a push-button bell. Now she placed the stick on that. When Tuna touched the stick, she got nothing. She touched it again. Still nothing. Tuna scrunched her brow and twitched her tail. Maybe if she twirled around. *DING!* Tuna accidentally touched the bell. Samantha gave her a bit of fish. It took several lessons before Tuna figured

out what Samantha
wanted her to do.

Finally, Samantha
gave Tuna a treat only if
she actually rang the bell.

DING! CLICK. Treat!

Now Tuna knew her first trick.

The cat purred all through her training.
Hmm, Samantha thought. *Tuna never used
to purr. This must make her happy.* Most of
the time Tuna was crabby. When
Samantha picked her up, Tuna clawed to
get down. If Samantha rubbed behind her
ears, Tuna shook her head and walked
away. But now Tuna came running when
Samantha blew her training whistle. She
quickly mastered trick after trick. "Tuna,
you're brilliant," Samantha told her.

But would Tuna perform for a crowd of people? There was one way to find out.

Samantha packed up Tuna's props. She wrote her name in glitter on the side of her pet carrier. Then she put Tuna inside and they left for California. They were going to a big fair where many pet lovers meet. Samantha could put Tuna's skills to the test there.

When they arrived at the fair, there were thousands of people strolling the grounds. Samantha lugged Tuna and her props through the crowd. She lugged them past a woolly poodle standing on a metal table. She lugged them past row upon row of big, heavy fish tanks. She lugged them past hamsters snoozing in metal cages. Samantha ignored them all. She needed to find the perfect spot for Tuna to perform.

Kitty "High Five"

You can train your cat to high-five. Ask your parents to buy a clicker and a bag of kitty treats at the pet store. Then sit on the floor with your cat. Hold the clicker in one hand. Grasp a treat between the fingers of your other hand. Now jiggle the treat in front of your cat. The second he swats for it, click and give him the treat. Do this over and over. Soon your kitty will slap you five whenever you click, even without a treat.

Aha! Samantha spied an empty countertop. She set Tuna's carrier down and called out to people walking past. "Hey!" she shouted. "Check out my cat. My cat needs a job."

A small crowd gathered. Samantha opened the pet carrier door and lured Tuna out with her favorite treat. The tricky kitty ignored all the people. She rang her bell. She rolled over. She jumped through a hoop. The crowd laughed and clapped, and Samantha grinned. What a cat! Tuna had what it takes. Maybe they would get lucky. Maybe Tuna would be discovered and become an actor.

Instead, a dog appeared.

Did You Know?

Like dogs, cats sweat through their paws.

Tuna froze. How dare this big mutt invade her space! Before Samantha could stop her, the cat leaped onto the dog's back. *EEEYOW!* She dug in her claws.

The dog whirled. Tuna screeched.

Fur flew as Samantha stood there in shock. Then as suddenly as everything started, it stopped. The fearless Tuna jumped back on the counter. Samantha stuffed her into her carrier and shut the door. The dog owner yanked his animal away.

After that Samantha put Tuna on a leash. She scheduled shows at libraries, schools, and birthday parties. These would not pay much. But at least Tuna would get some practice. Samantha prayed that their big break would come soon.

Head down, paws tucked in, Tuna soars over the hurdles.

Chapter 2

Lights, Camera, ACTION!

Tuna loved performing, but it cost a lot of money to travel to shows. Samantha couldn't earn much at other jobs because Tuna took up almost all her time. Samantha didn't know how much longer she could keep it up. Then one day, she got an exciting phone call.

"I found your number on the Internet," the speaker said. "I'm looking for a cat actor." The voice belonged to a college student in Florida named Dana Buning. Dana was making a short movie for a class assignment. It was a scary movie called *Zeke* (sounds like ZEEK). It starred a man and his cat.

"Are you paying?" Samantha asked.

"Yes. We have a production budget," said Dana.

"We'll do it!" Samantha said with joy.

"Not so fast," Dana said. "Four other cats are trying out for the part. I need to see what Tuna can do."

Dana sent Samantha the script. Tuna was to play the bad guy. First off she had to look angry. That was easy. Tuna was naturally cranky. But she also needed to lick her mouth on cue. She had to snarl and pretend to bite. She had to lie flat on her back with her front legs stretched over her head. She needed to stay that way while other actors performed around her.

Samantha didn't know if Tuna would be okay sitting still for a big, scary camera on wheels. This role needed a brave cat.

Samantha decided that they would go for it. She taught Tuna to do everything the film needed. Tuna caught on fast.

Soon it was time to show the world Tuna's new tricks. Samantha had her perform for free to get her used to acting in strange places. The more shows Tuna did, the braver she got. Samantha recorded the shows and sent the videos to Florida. Dana studied them carefully. One day she called Samantha.

Yippee! Tuna got the part!

"The other cats are too nice," Dana said. "We like Tuna because she looks evil."

Two trips to Florida followed. Tuna worked hard. When the movie was done, she appeared in almost every scene.

Samantha was proud of her cat. She expected to hear from Hollywood any day.

But months passed and the phone didn't ring. "Don't worry, Tuna," Samantha said. "You'll get your chance. Just wait and see."

Tuna just blinked.

Samantha started taking the cat to a monthly film festival. She handed out flyers and set up a folding table to showcase Tuna. Sometimes show business people attended these movies. Maybe one of them would need a cat actor and Tuna would land another movie role.

In the meantime, Samantha taught Tuna to pluck a tiny guitar. One night, Samantha took the cat to a dinner theater. Dishes were clattering. People were talking. A hired band was playing in the next room. Samantha wondered if Tuna would perform.

But when she opened Tuna's carrier, hooray! The furry musician ran straight to her guitar. Tuna played like she was the only performer in the place.

Samantha had an idea. *I'll form an all-cat band,* she decided. She already had tiny instruments left over from her goose, duck, and chicken act. All she had to do was train some more cats to play them.

Did You Know?

In ancient Egypt, cats were made into mummies after they died.

The trouble was that Samantha's new cats were not like Tuna. Dakota, Pinky, and Nue jammed it up big time at home. But take them out in public? The scaredy-cats hid in their carriers.

Samantha wondered why the cats were so afraid. What could she do to make them feel safe? She tried offering different treats. That didn't work. Maybe she should ditch the band and form a duo with Tuna and just one other cat. That didn't work either.

Somehow Samantha had to make different performance spaces feel the same. Finally, she had an idea. She bought a sheet of soft vinyl (sounds like VINE-el) floor covering. At home she laid it out on her kitchen table and set up the band instruments on top. The cats got used to feeling the soft plastic under their feet.

When Samantha did a show, she rolled up the floor and took it with her.

Now the floor felt the same wherever they went. "They step on that," Samantha said, "and everything is okay."

One night she placed an ad on the Internet. "I have a Cat Circus act," she typed. "We need a place to perform."

A few days later, Samantha turned on her computer and bingo! A local art gallery was offering her space. She brought the roll of vinyl flooring and a cloth backdrop. The cats felt at home and played like rock stars.

People loved them. Soon other places invited them to perform.

Homeless No More

Animal shelters are full of unwanted cats and kittens. They can't hold any more. So many cats are put to death. This upsets Samantha. She saves lives by bringing kittens home and teaching them tricks.

Then she shows them off on stage. People clap and cheer. Some people ask to adopt the cats.

Samantha has found forever homes for 85 kittens. One of them is really special. She plays piano. "Whenever her owners come home," Samantha says, "she plays them a song!"

Samantha named her band The Rock Cats. They were the only all-cat band in America. The four meowers began playing several shows a week. Samantha crossed her fingers. She still believed that they could make it big if the right people noticed them.

One night a dog trainer called. He was somebody she had met two years earlier at the pet fair.

"A theater in Branson, Missouri, had an animal show booked," he said. "But the act backed out. I suggested they hire you to fill in."

"Branson! Wow!" Samantha pumped her fist in the air. She jumped up and down.

"Yahoo! Wake up, Tuna," she yelled. "This could be it—our big break!"

A special guest performs with the Rock Cats. Who knew a chicken could play tambourine?

Samantha and her assistant loaded heavy props into her old van. The last items they packed were pet carriers. These held 13 cats, a chicken, and a groundhog. Samantha had created an hour-long show. It included the Rock Cats band and a circus act called the Acro-Cats.

Just outside Branson, Samantha saw a billboard for a top-hatted man with many cats. It was world-famous Popovich (sounds like POP-OH-VITCH).

Come show time, hundreds of people poured into the theater. Workers passed out programs saying that the Rock Cats were replacing Popovich's Cat Circus. The audience was not happy. They had come to see Popovich.

Samantha felt nervous as she peeked out from behind the curtain. It was very tense backstage. There were two other animal acts. One of the trainers complained that Samantha's cats were after his birds. The other one hated Samantha's jumble of props.

Even Samantha's cats felt nervous.

The curtain went up. Samantha carried Tuna out on stage. Uh-oh! The furry superstar forgot her part. Tuna was supposed to open the show by pushing a lever that turned on a light. Instead, she chewed a foil bow stuck on a prop. "Your light, Tuna," Samantha urged. "Go to your light."

Tuna strolled over and lazily touched the lever. Nothing happened. Tuna started back toward her carrier.

The audience shifted in their seats.

"Tuna," Samantha said and motioned with her finger.

Tuna came halfway. She stretched and groomed herself.

"TUNA!" Samantha's face burned. Finally Tuna did what she was told. The light shone.

But it got worse. During their number, Dakota suddenly stopped drumming. "Phsssssssst!" Her snarling bandmate swatted her.

It was a cat fight! On stage. In front of the crowd.

Tuna lifted her head, but she didn't join in. She quit ringing her bell. She used her paw to wash her face.

Samantha covered her eyes. "It's awful," she moaned. "Our show stinks."

The man who booked the Rock Cats took Samantha aside. "Get a costume," he told her. "Learn to go with the flow. When the cats go crazy, crack a joke."

Samantha nodded. But inside she worried. *Maybe I should get a normal job,* she thought.

Finally, this job was over. Samantha loaded up the van.

While Samantha drove home to Chicago, Tuna sat beside her with her back turned. Samantha knew better than to pet the cat. But she liked her company. She remembered Tuna's "killer stare" in the movie *Zeke*. She pictured the kitty ringing her bell on stage. And she thought about her long list of tricks.

Tuna is very smart, Samantha reminded herself. *She loves to perform. And she may be the best cat actress in America.*

Samantha smiled and straightened her back. She would keep trying.

For the next five years Samantha and her cats hit the road. They played art galleries and small theaters. With every show, Samantha got better with the audience.

Tuna didn't need to improve. She was already great.

Now it was spring 2012. The Acro-Cats were booked in a 500-seat theater in Santa Fe, New Mexico! That was almost as big as the theater in Branson. Samantha was so excited.

But Thursday night most of the seats were empty.

Even so, Tuna's performance was terrific. She ruled the stage!

Word spread. The crowd got bigger on Friday and Saturday. Then came Sunday.

Good Luck Cat

In Japan, people put a statue of a cat in their front window. It is called Maneki Neko (sounds like MA-NECK-EE NECK-O). It looks like a sitting cat waving goodbye. Except in Japan that kind of wave means, "Come here."

The statue reminds people of a pet cat said to have saved a man's life. People love that old story. And they use Maneki Neko as a good luck charm. Does it work? Probably not. But it honors cats, which is lucky for them.

A line of people stretched down the block. Grandmothers with walkers. Long-haired men in tie-dyed T-shirts. Girls in flip-flops. And young couples pushing strollers. Fifteen minutes before show time, the theater sold out.

Inside, the stage looked like a cat playground. Circus stools, tightropes, hurdles, ramps, and a crawl-through tube stood ready. Tiny instruments sat in front of a red curtain sprinkled with stars.

Lively music played. Samantha walked onstage. She wore a black cat suit and felt cat ears. "Here's Tuna!" she announced.

The furry superstar trotted out wearing a sparkly collar. She turned on her light. She stood on her hind legs and flipped open a welcome sign. Other cats entered.

They walked the high wire, rode skateboards, and climbed ropes.

The delighted crowd "oohed" and "aahed."

Now came the grand finale—the Rock Cats. "We have Pinky on guitar," Samantha said. "Dakota is on drums, and it's Nue on keyboard." She pointed to Tuna sitting down front with her upraised paw. "Tuna plays cowbell."

Samantha waved a stick and the "concert" began. These cool cats could not read music. And the sound they made? Better cover your ears. "They are a little tone deaf," said Samantha, smiling. "But they do all play together."

No sooner did Samantha speak than Dakota stopped playing. She ducked behind her drum. She looked like she was about to run off the stage.

Samantha knew what to do. She turned to the audience and grinned. "Cats want to be paid," she said. Then she handed Dakota a piece of chicken.

Dakota started the beat again and the audience cheered.

Then Tuna took over once more. She rang her bell and tapped her tip jar.

The crowd laughed out loud. Dozens of fans came to the stage and dropped in tips.

Tuna and the Rock Cats had finally done it. They had made the big time.

EEEE-YOW!

THE END

DON'T MISS!

NATIONAL GEOGRAPHIC **KIDS** **CHAPTERS**

APE ESCAPES!

And More True Stories of Animals Behaving Badly

By Aline Alexander Newman

NATIONAL GEOGRAPHIC

**Turn the page
for a sneak preview . . .**

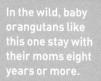
In the wild, baby orangutans like this one stay with their moms eight years or more.

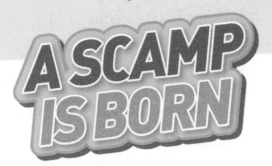

A SCAMP IS BORN

July 1965, Omaha, Nebraska

A young orangutan peers out of his cage at the Henry Doorly Zoo. No humans are in sight. The coast is clear.

He sticks his long fingers through the chain-link fence. He bends back one corner. He pulls. *ZZIIIIP!* The stiff metal fencing unravels like a hand-knit scarf.

Some time later, veterinarian Lee Simmons arrives at work. He rounds a bend in the path and *yikes!* Dr. Simmons stops in his tracks. It couldn't be, but it is. A shaggy, red-haired ape sits up in a tree. *How did he get loose?*

The ape is about six years old, tailless, and weighs 100 pounds (45 kg). He has a mustache and beard like a famous movie character. For that reason he is called Fu Manchu. Fu's arms are super strong and longer than most fourth graders are tall. In a wrestling match against a man, the orangutan would win.

The ape doesn't move or make a sound. But Dr. Simmons sees a twinkle in his eyes. The vet can't help but wonder if Fu knew what he was doing. *It's like he's been sitting there just waiting for me.*

Fu climbs down. The sun sparkles on his red hair as he scrambles back to his cage. Dr. Simmons follows, shaking his head. *What a crazy ape!* He locks Fu inside. He calls someone to fix the fence and then goes about his normal business. And Fu goes about his—dreaming up more hijinks to come.

Fu was born in a rain forest on the Indonesian island of Sumatra (sounds like SUE-MAH-TRA). Like most baby orangutans, Fu probably never knew his father. Orangutan mothers care for their helpless babies. Fu's mother nursed him. She held him and snuggled him. Every night she built them a nest high in the treetops.

These sleeping nests were the size of bathtubs. Fu's mother made them by twisting leafy branches together. Each fresh, new nest must have felt as comfy to Fu as clean bedsheets do to you.

Usually Fu and his mom stayed dry in their cozy bed in the sky. At other times thunder boomed. Rain fell in sheets. Then the apes huddled together and turned giant leaves into umbrellas.

During the day, Fu often rode on his mother's back. He clutched her hair as they swung through the trees looking for durian (sounds like DUR-EE-ANN) fruits. Durian fruits stink like sweaty gym socks. But orangutans go ape for the smelly stuff.

The problem is durian fruits don't all ripen at the same time, and the trees are scattered. To find them, orangutans must keep a map of the forest inside their heads. For Fu's mother it must have been like memorizing a school bus route with hundreds of stops.

Finding water was easier. It collects in hollow tree trunks after a rain. Fu might have gotten a drink by scooping water out with a folded leaf. Or maybe he chewed leaves into a sort of sponge. Then he sopped up water and dripped it into his mouth. Either way, Fu used leaves as tools.

Long ago, Indonesian people dubbed these clever apes "orangutans."

Did You Know?

As baby orangutans get older, they ride "piggyback" to get a better view of their surroundings.

In their language the word *orang* means "person" and *utan* means "forest." Together you get "person of the forest."

One day Fu and his mother heard strange sounds in the swamp. Hunters had entered the jungle. They carried axes and homemade nets on their backs. Rivers of sweat ran down the men's bare chests. Armies of insects buzzed in their faces. But nothing stopped them. The men were animal collectors. They feed their families by catching and selling wild animals. A baby orangutan will get them a lot of money.

Did Fu's mother know they wanted her baby? Probably not, but she sensed danger. She swung from limb to limb, snapping off branches. She threw the branches down on the hunters.

The animal collectors looked up. The mother ape looked like a tiny black doll hanging against the blue sky. Was she holding a baby?

The hunters had a traditional way of catching orangutans. They didn't try to climb up after them. Not at first. That might have spooked the ape into escaping through the treetops. Instead, the animal collectors formed a circle. They pulled out their axes and hacked away at tree trunks.

The ground shook as a tall tree crashed to the forest floor. Then a second one, and a third. The trees were so close together that each one that fell knocked down another. CHOP! CHOP! The men worked their way to the last tree—the one holding the apes.

Want to know what happens next?
Be sure to check out *Ape Escapes!* Available
wherever books and ebooks are sold.

INDEX

MORE INFORMATION

To find more information about the animal species featured in this book, check out these books and websites:

Cats vs. Dogs, National Geographic, 2011

National Geographic Kids Everything Dogs, National Geographic, 2012

National Geographic "Animals: Domestic Cat"
animals.nationalgeographic.com/animals/mammals/domestic-cat

National Geographic "Animals: Domestic Dog"
animals.nationalgeographic.com/animals/mammals/domestic-dog

National Geographic "Animals: Groundhog"
animals.nationalgeographic.com/animals/mammals/groundhog

Dunkirk Dave website and videos
www.dunkirkdave.com

Rock Cats and Acro-Cats website and videos
www.circuscats.com

This book is dedicated to my grandchildren,
Hannah and Chase,
who will always be superstars in my eyes.

CREDITS

4–5, AP Images/Chris Carlson; 6, AP Images/Chris Carlson; 15, Joyce Marrero/Shutterstock; 16, AP Images/Chris Carlson; 23, Alaska Photography/Getty Images; 26, AP Images/Chris Carlson; 35, Adogslifephoto/Dreamstime; 36–37, © A. Neil Newman; 38, © A. Neil Newman; 44, © A. Neil Newman; 48, © A. Neil Newman; 55, Petr Mašek/Dreamstime; 58, © A. Neil Newman; 64, © A. Neil Newman; 68–69, © Steve Grubman; 70, © Steve Grubman; 77, Linn Currie/Shutterstock; 80, Courtesy Smantha Martin; 88, © Marmaduke St. John/Alamy; 90, © Joy Schmoll; 97, J. Helgason/Shutterstock; 101, Cyril Ruoso/Biosphoto; 102, Life on White/Alamy; 102 (Background), © Elena Elisseeva/Dreamstime; 111, AP Images/Chris Carlson; COVER, AP Images/Chris Carlson

ACKNOWLEDGMENTS

A special thank you to:

My ever-helpful husband, Neil, for taking such great groundhog pictures

Bob Will and Bill Verge, devoted groundhog rescuers

Samantha Martin, owner and manager of The Rock Cats

Michael Schelin, best friend of Opee, the Motocross Pup

Hope Irvin Marston, Judy Ann Grant, and Jule Lattimer, the members of my writers' group

Becky Baines, project editor, National Geographic Children's Books

About the author: www.alinealexandernewman.com